the Light

Searching for the Light

Matthew James Ould

Paper Doll

Published by Paper Doll
Hutton Close
South Church
Bishop Auckland
Co. Durham
DL14 6XB

ISBN: 1 86248 151 2

Typeset by CBS, Martlesham Heath,
Ipswich, Suffolk
Printed by Lintons Printers, Co. Durham

To family and friends

CONTENTS

What Was I Before	1
Mother	2
Approaching Marriage Day	4
We Must Be Punished	5
Father	7
Afternoon Scenes	9
They Said It Was Only A Field	10
Let's Talk Democracy	12
Paganism - The Old And The New	14
Lost	16
Jealousy Is Trying To Leave	17
Hello Special Friend	19
Playing With Fire	21
The Healers	23
The Magic Cottage	25
Hail The Trees	27
My First Child's Just Been Born	29
I've Been Drinking Too Long	31
Everyone Needs Friends	32
The Golden Soul	34
Computers Are Good But—	36
I Remember That Precious Weekend	37
Crash	39
Imagine Going To War	40
Roll The Dice Please, One More Time For Me	41
Money - My Rise And Fall	43
Lonely And Rarely Sad, I Thought	45
Actor's Memories	47

Out Of Work	48
Messages In The Weather	49
I Cannot Believe I Nearly Gave This Away	51
Lives Are Easier When Love's Around	53
The Old And Time	55

WHAT WAS I BEFORE (A POEM ON A PAST LIFE)

She trod this earth five hundred years ago,
the village woman whom love partnerships eluded.
The deepest lay in her Profession,
a herbalist which bred hallmarks of frustration.

The authorities suspiciously smelt the scent
and sought to weave her within their web.
'Herbalism is a terminal oddity,
overseas, this creature would be earmarked a witch.
England (tut-tut) is far too soft a haven!'

Her premature departure at twenty-two was sickness.
She escaped the feared judicial noose,
the wise woman's presence/profession lingered in the village,
like filtering down herbalistic lore.
Work aimed to cure,
thus both eyes closed content.

MOTHER

'Mother, thanks for healing my mind,'
when I saw stars fall from the sky
and for producing magical moments,
to be recalled in periods of sadness,
always on a crest of a wave.

My largest promise is to send you
the letter that ends all my other ones,
thanking you for all you have done.
Yet words do not come easy to me
and time slips by farther every day.

Sorry for the year my words turned against you,
moving from town to town produced no love
    fairytale,
the greatest love always stemmed from you.
I mentally grabbed your shadow when alone,
hours of time on the telephone
helped stem the flow of tears.

Your constant supplies of strength
are a great motto to me.
You never know what is around the corner,
those words keep coming around again to me.
We are lucky to have stuck together as a team.

The generation gap no longer seems that much
and love through kind words is the saviour now,
so do not be scared to ever run to me for help.
I will always be there for you
that is the beauty of loving somebody forever.

So Mother I wrote this poem for you this evening
as a tribute to your kind soul.
Your love for people again and again
will always keep candles burning,
when somebody feels they are trapped in the cold.
Goodnight Mother; faith and love, these are treasures to me.

APPROACHING MARRIAGE DAY

Her voice of autumn suddenly gripped her
and symbolically shredded snaps of past desires.
Her lover's personality seemingly could not spout
faint breezes in a well-groomed tree,
yet feared their secret viper moods
would sprint and pierce the precious gift of time.

Sometimes she sensed her body leaving her
and being enlightened with her favourite flower.
Then she grasped her boyfriend's voice pleading,
'I would be stuck in permanent rain,
if your entire image was not entwined in my brain.'

She imagined their binding day
on their sacred local football ground.
In the stands, rejuvenated people stand tall,
whose Marriage shadows had closed in,
singing joyfully 'Give marriage a chance,
Regardless of the times.'
The sun will always take a bow.

Let's walk, talk and love on thin air,
the Wedding day harmony blues may plead
for lingering survival on thin air,
yet we cannot blossom on thin air.
Let's free fall quickly from thin air,
otherwise we'll be lost in our dream cloud.

WE MUST BE PUNISHED

The premier lash cascaded me to heaven and back,
this daily dose of ecstasy outweighs most people's thrills.
It's divine retribution for the sin I have committed,
each stroke summons pleasant images of my wife,
whom I departed for my daughter's best friend
and she administers my planned object of desire.

Miss Whiplash cried out lines of adultery,
from the Old and the New Testament.
Every time you quote incorrectly,
a fragment of your heart dies,
and your wife's picture grows ever more blurred.

My son's best friend delivers a curious portrait,
when we say 'how's it going?' on the step.
My wife's beaten black and blue, then confronts me
and deals the ultimate ace.
'This was my seventh day of suffering,
since we cut the scissors together
of the picture which says:
You're together until somebody's dust,
by the way, this is my replacement',
Then I knelt down and confessed all.

It was a curious scenario,
'We expected the post mortem,' cried our children.
'No my dears, we are now reunited.
Early on in our marriage we granted
each other an openness to anybody,
but only for the first year.'
Unscrupulous behaviour will return to haunt thee,
exchanging the same dream recently.
'So, please children, turn the tables
and tell your elders, this is how to behave.'

FATHER

One of these days we must sit down
and discuss what we don't understand about
each other.
It's going to be hard for we are both shy
and I pray it won't be long.
Yet recent events giving answers
may have ended that for a while.

It was very hard you changing jobs after many
years,
in my mind you struck gold
many times on your work journey in life.
Some work methods I've tried to copy
and these will stay to my retirement hopefully.

We share a lot of interests
luckily some returned to me recently,
because otherwise it would have been sad
to have thought of the joy they gave us
and never to touch our hearts again.

Your courage with facing certain problems
is a tribute to you as a human being.
Stay brave, things seem so much better now,
you led the team when we were in despair,
your determination repaired our jaded minds.

As the years float on by,
your gentle manner will always help you.
You taught us life spares nobody from problems.
Lessons of life I learn from you
which one day I would be proud
to pass on to my children.

AFTERNOON SCENES

Daffodils and marigolds chattering – laughing,
they're blowing in the wind.
Honey bees drop onto them,
falling fragments out of the sky.
Lovely lawn – it's just lost its beards.
Behind – the golden eagle hovers around
that small mountain den.
'My territory – that's sacred,
trespassers thou will be pecked'.

Friends and lovers smile into each other's eyes,
'Who is really there?'
Cobras and charmers perfecting perfect patterns
for tomorrow's enchanted child.
Middle-aged man, hat, pipe, polly on his left,
Stares blankly into the sky.
Is it the clouds/his incredible career
veering into another phase?
Daughter, mother, Gran and Grandpa George,
link arms – tango into the midsummer's fading
light.

As night time falls, closing time please,
people gone, flowers sleep and I must go now
too.

THEY SAID IT WAS ONLY A FIELD

The Family huddled around wrestling with fate,
our field, three hundred years of heritage
duped by some town schmuck.
The storm of '29 seemingly engulfed your
Grandfather,
yet he was already married to his earth,
so wavered not when the moon broke down,
the field interacted with his soul.

Some locals speculated our field produce
could inject social harmony to
the pleading starving town masses.
When famine acquainted itself in the village,
other fields were readily employable,
yet even the worms fled in disgust.
So the families wallowed in self-contentment
by queuing for life from our field,
they voted it the saviour that year.

The prospects of viewing concrete over lambs
flooded out our house with tears.
Residing in town is a one-way lair
to a crockload of despair.
I swore my ashes would be scattered
over the field, the town doesn't own them.

The cock crowed 13, signalling our demise,
for traitor was reportedly initialling the deed,
sunbathing sipping champagne in that field.

But the villagers arrived with sparkling eyes,
the petition signalled victory
for country over town.
Our bloodline seemingly dormant,
now oozed from every grain.
Thank you comrades,
come share the fine feast from our field.

LET'S TALK DEMOCRACY

Our son is snared in his shell,
muted by the racial taunts.
Yet his parents applauded
the country they lived in.
Self-humbling meetings took place,
when tormentors and victims met face to face.

Some tormentors blamed their country's colonial
past,
the imperial attitude was 'We will
always be better than you.'
Thus although the empire is redundant,
this standard pathetic colonial thought
has taught us to react
in some of the old format.

The mediators squashed this notion 'It's too easy
to blame our country's Ancestral past.'
They said it's really about lessons
being dug from the human heart
and letting harmony in,
for peace will reign when harmony wins.

After several meetings the rejoicing
parents penetrated their son's shell.
'Hoorah' his stature is rising high
and feels his confidence is everywhere.
The three of us now campaign
for more meetings across the country,
for it's our land as well,
lets talk harmony – that's democracy.

PAGANISM – THE OLD AND THE NEW

I, Rufus King of England will soon die, it's 1100
AD.
Oh, unsuspecting friend did you release this
arrow?
Yet these woods cannot hide all my foes.
The public were persistently painted a picture
of how evil my mind was,
however the propaganda machine never stopped
rolling,
because I am openly Pagan.

King Rufus said 'It's now half a Millennium
since Paganism was purged from these shores
I tried to stand up and show my people
that the older religion of a country
can live in harmony with the new.'

Nine hundred years then passed by,
when a mere tourist observing Rufus's final port
of call,
reckoned the king is smiling,
for more people now say openly
'Paganism, I really do believe'
and fearing less the heavy intolerant hand.

The tourist pictured Rufus's ideal scene,
a group of believers, critics and sceptics share
    common ground,
'Toleration – not fundamentalism, is the key.
Old and new Religions and non-believers please
    unite
and be a blueprint for evermore.'

LOST

Two ants scurried across the table,
pet rat snored silently,
telephones alive – sorry it's in the mind.
The aspirins seemingly hover nervously
saying 'Surely not again?'

She left 66 days ago,
seems like 666.
Mates rapping, tapping on the front,
they're avoiding my frequent distant stare.

'Gotta be some way out of here,'
(in French) to the hanging masks on the wall
which surrounds me so much more,
from it,
hundreds of hands – flap – clap – flap.

Leapt up,
counted sheep to sleep.
Lovely Lucille appears in the night,
then I wake once more.

JEALOUSY IS TRYING TO LEAVE

People breathed with new souls again
the night jealousy died.
There were many shrines destroyed
in people's minds by jealousy.
Faces seemed brighter and more welcoming,
the moment jealousy crept from town.
Arguments were more pleasant, even the moon
smiled
when jealousy was bankrupt from the dictionary.

Happy faces were soon drinking tears,
when jealousy soon returned
and the air seemed heavier with remorse again.
Flowers seemed cross to go into people's homes
in case they smelt the scent of jealousy.
Everyone is joining forces, stating unity in the
town,
to ban jealousy for permanent time.

A stranger stalked through town the other night
and promised a 'no-lose' windfall for the town,
It promised it knew the secret of expelling
jealousy for good.
The dancing was for one week, nobody dared
sleep
as jealousy packed up to haunt other minds.
Yet everyone became suddenly too nice
and some people even got bored.
Jealousy just did not know how to leave.

The last waltz on a Sunday night in town,
is held to remind the town of jealousy,
that the human soul can never rid of it
and although nobody would admit it,
everybody owned a piece of it.
People wrote down jealous thoughts and swapped it
with the neighbours, so lessons were learnt.

In a generation, the stranger will return
to see how much jealousy can go away.
So the flower of peace returns to remind people
of a possible permanent joy, when jealousy said 'Goodbye'.

HELLO SPECIAL FRIEND

My mind drifted towards you the other day,
although it's so less often now.
Have you found that long awaited love?
Or are you in some lonely place in the rain?
Your voice seems a fading memory now.

I always knew your many friends
gave you heartfelt advice when you were down.
It must seem that I only desired
to know you to secure romance.
I called to express sincere thoughts,
yet you were lost in the town crowd
to find a precious welcome escape.

Perhaps when we are in different places,
sometimes we remember each other's images,
    thinking
'What they would say to help?'
Do a few tears escape remembering
we said we'd stay special friends.
So should I prepare for a tearful reunion?
Or see your image float from the shore
with happiness beating on you from the sun.

As Valentine days fly past,
will your face lose its grasp on me?
Your picture of flowers in my room
will always shine brightly with happy memories.

Dream on, dream on, yet I
don’t want to escape the past,
but who can replace that special friend?

PLAYING WITH FIRE
(OUIJA BOARD)

I really was a sceptic scornful of the board,
the dangers were outlined yet the invitation was
    always there,
temptation finally prevailed as we battered down
    the sacred doors,
the glass buzzed around and we recorded all.

A tale of pregnancy and murder last century
transported us into the other world,
yet what scene/re-enactment-fantasy were we
    playing out?
The language was contemporary,
whose tortured souls had we restored?

Alarm bells rang when
we were nearly stuck to the glass and our chairs.
My mentor became our tormentor and then slid
    into reverse.
A strange stench hung in the room
and a picture was seemingly lopsided,
exhausted by the event.

The next few days I walked between the living
    and the dead,
examples please – well, a woman's face was
demonic in the crowd
and smoke filtered into my personal domain.

Medication restored my balance several days
later,
yet four hundred on I was consulting with a
Priest.
The door of freedom may slam shut for good
if I elect to choose much time
in the presence of the dead.

THE HEALERS

There are many hurdles for me to jump
before fleeing this deep draining illness
and the tablets are letting me down.
However I will not fold my arms,
sit down and say a final goodbye.

My body wanted to become its former self,
so I walked daily in the countryside.
There were deer who crept up to me
and raised me a big hearty smile.
The knees became weak for I knew
good people were also saying fond 'hello',
I must be stronger willed before them.

There's a rustling by the brook,
an owl is yelling out 'I'm in trouble'.
Thus I pick up the mantle
of being the strong one,
I had preserved a life that day.

Yet it was largely the medicine
which made it fly once again.
So I rushed to the cupboard
like old Mother Hubbard,
who would never have run out of medicine.

Thus I took up retaking my medicine
and moved house to the countryside.

Again and again it cried out to me
'Here you can regain to train
to claim back a new lease of life.'

The old walks lifted me more than ever,
but first I had paid my respects
to a sad old ailing tree,
yet now it stood teeming with life,
so rested by it with a happy heart.

However in closing this chapter,
I must pay tribute to the real healers,
the medicine and people
who have assisted me
to regain that precious gift called life.

THE MAGIC COTTAGE

The cottage illuminates the soul's greatest fantasy,
entrenched in the vaults of the forest,
where even spiders get puzzled finding the address.
There's always a blanket of harmony waiting,
even the fairies and the wolves exchange
delicate words when meeting in the cottage.

It usually snows to match your most recent dream
of the most tranquil scene of the cottage.
It feels its beauty melting unless a person's
passion does not increase tenfold when stumbling upon it.
Please remember, this house traps your mind,
hearts are not forgiven when viewing then stalking away.

The last few owners were healers of people and animals,
using the forest's natural gifts so love is ingrained
in the cottage walls, moonlight quarrels won't spoil it.
The princess and prince of all seasons always visit,
to bless this cottage with picturesque seasonal scenes.

They think only owners who summon dodos
out of
the finest trees around the cottage should breathe
here.
Yet everyone has magic in the palm of their hands
to conjure up the cottage visions when alone and
sad.

The cottage owners must see heavens and beauty
in everything,
otherwise the solitude could reduce sanity to
dust.
The cottage will dissolve in tears if money is
given for it.
The cottage passes on the secret to new owners
in a dream, of the life-saving medicine
to the forest's rarest find, the unicorns.

The cottage's emotions are ablaze with joy,
for it knows a dream has entered someone's mind
of the paradise cottage. The location
where every person wants to stay.
The people's dream escape.

HAIL THE TREES

Signs of a harmonious infectious Eden,
with people and forests ignited, when
humans invited the tree spirits
to unite with their souls.
The dispute had not flared then.

Centuries later people shared visions,
the sun had turned green
and it's suicidal – it's going to explode.
Some people forgot their past green sins,
chop chop more more cannot stop.

Humankind crawled off to see the spirit people
and with honest regret snared on their tongues,
bowed down handing a fresh gold olive leaf.
Seemingly stagnant statues suddenly saw sense,
both leaders' tortured breath waned with talks,
to prove the sun would go sane again.

The spirit people welcomed them
to a long buried show.
Ancient Ancestors showing how their skills
respected the 'hearts' of the forest.
The forest's black-eyed dogs started
planning, gnawing the humans' brains,
dishing deserved retribution for destroying trees.

The dogs turned friendly seeing
humans with tears in their eyes,
for the environmental demonstration
was not set in year 'zero',
it was in AD 2222.
In many places around the globe,
creatures and humans were breathing freer
for the trees were plentiful again.

MY FIRST CHILD'S JUST BEEN BORN

I must not stare into
my first-born child's eyes,
to ponder if they have
the potential killer traits.

I want to collect a silver moon,
the timeless lucky emblem for my child
to emotionally use carefully as my first gift.
The words 'think lucky' would
always be enshrined on it.
The whirlpool of harm then won't
embrace the infant for a flickering moment.
Are the armies of protection already too stoked?

The nurse said generously 'You are thirty-two'.
No, I am twenty-three, I look older
because I sell flowers near Heaven's gate.
One metes out honest sympathy,
working near the cemetery,
as delicately as a surgeon with the scalpel.

I feel like reserving a place
dealing overtime with the Reaper
for the last seven years.
I also cope with personal demons slating me
for having an abortion aged sixteen.

The night I met my child
equalled my rebirth
and once again the flowers
had plenty to say.
The drain near my flower stall
cast away my entrenched swarms of tears.

The dead embraced the new born in a dream
and wished them well on earth.
So many happy vibes fixated in my head,
for my offspring had awarded me a
radiant new pathway in my life.

I'VE BEEN DRINKING TOO LONG

Seven pints yesterday
will the nightmare never cease?
Morrison-Moon I won't follow you.
Friends galore evaporated in the picture
even my mother – 'not you too!'

Poe drunk from bar – bar,
Forty's young, yet celebrated through and
through.
What about idiot? (That's myself)
as the sick crashed the wall,
enjoyed the 90s – what about 2?

Drinking – silently sinking,
blinking up, now down and out.
'Six foot under – only twenty-eight,'
roared an ex-drunkard, now controlled
realisation triggered through the brain.

Choice is yours

'Friends forever
v
Drink & Die!'

EVERYONE NEEDS FRIENDS

Friends smile brighter than rare groomed diamonds,
memories of my visions of anger fade when
moonlight reveals friends against the sparkle of one's mind.
Cascades of tears are jilted by remembering friend's kind words,
telephone wires melt with frenzy when gusts
of sound advice sing loud along the line.
Phrases from friends' letters are strewn in the brain,
I hope my name's initialled over a friend's heart.

I am like a rare animal who hibernates a long time,
then when a friend cannot dispose of bad luck,
my words aim to strike heavier chords than optimistic dreams.
The message aims to rock-a-bye the friend's soul,
that would be recalled until they surrender life.
My role is to repair friends' sad states without paybacks,
I am blunt, no midnight soft words trail my lips.
My mind stops clocks 24 hours a day when friends shout help.

Friends seemed lost by you not uttering 'sorry'.
You know they are gone when their dreams don't excuse you.

The investment was heavy, you climbed many
mountains together,
they dig in the memory which time does not
remove.
Well, go on, lose face, but this victory's for life,
for you've kept a friend by remembering hard
times together,
when the ties were so strong hurricanes could
not remove them,
but most importantly rock-a-bye the word
'sorry' to your friend
and a new dawn will seem fresh again.

THE GOLDEN SOUL

Whenever I view your smiling face,
I almost bow down in praise,
for the time you helped me
when my husband was ill.
You were my best friend
and this I will take to the grave.

I have worked all over the world
and kept a record of how kind people are,
your score is the highest one.
I'm much older now, I've stopped the records,
you've won the trophy of golden soul,
I feel that 'thank you' is not enough.

It's been over thirty years since we last met,
but your smiling face still throws away harsh winds.
I have kept a photo of it,
to help myself when in dark corners.
Your smiling face saved your wondering mind
from whispered abuses of the humankind.

So it's your actions such as smiling,
that seem to save people you befriend.
My words sometimes do melt people,
yet sometimes they are simply not enough.
It's a golden soul I want to keep
for myself to fight on in life.

So if you ever own a golden soul,
always keep a tight hold on it
and people will never tire of you.
I'm moving now to a brand new place,
still looking for another golden soul.
Yet as time rapidly passes by
I say to myself, 'Nobody's perfect'.
Shall I give up? for overall I feel fine.

COMPUTERS ARE GOOD BUT—

Mum is this really true?
Children of my age used to play
many games in village streets.
You purchased my best buddy
at only sixteen working hours.
No human would ever locate
all these pals for someone
as reclusive as myself.
Goodbyes are far less painful,
a button's pressed, you've never met their face.

My brain's aghast, I love assisting the human
race,
but again 'They've purchased most of my wares'
said an optician sadly, recalling
a professor's correct utterance
that new human ailments are breeding fast.
I wind myself up repeating the same old rhyme,
their evening relaxation is adding to their pain,
in front of the knackered square box.
They confess 'Well, I don't watch much,'
but then forget what their day job was.

I REMEMBER THAT PRECIOUS WEEKEND

Recently I bought a caravan,
took my children to the sea.
My wife stayed alone at home,
would have thought tensions flew around,
yet everyone was happy all the time.

Only my wife before stopped mayhem in my mind,
now the children helped me in ways I did not know.
I was easily the weakest person,
now life's stars seem to sparkle more,
the weekend addressed questions buried long ago.

My wife was able to go dancing with friends,
said she felt younger and was free,
which I will try and remember every day.
Women's rights must boom much more here.
Talking more about deep feelings which must arise.

My world now collides with greater joy,
when the house welcomes her home.
Many meetings of hearts and minds
have made us feel more free.
There's something in the way we react to words
that produce magical moments to treasure.
It's like a second honeymoon for us.

The sun could vanish, I would notice,
if she left me for good all alone.
Yet we are coping much better now,
for we know we will always
be opposite in so many ways.
I respect her hopefully, so not to sound demeaning.
Our lives are so much better now, since that weekend.

CRASH

Two seconds to react,
screams are trapped in one's throat.
The car and ourselves seem weighted by chains,
as time dies before car-car contact.
My eyes shut down to kill the haunting scene,
but dream time imagery will conjure up
?   ?   ?

Reality returns, strange forces emerge
swarming around the car, it's the living dead!
I yell,
'Have any passengers left this earth?'
Everybody's ok,
ordeal's over and we can now just walk away.

Flashing lights shatter the myth that everything's
    normal,
Inside the ambulance it feels like one's final port
    of call.
I'm soon discharged and drift home to bed,
somebody's saying 'Tomorrow's just another
    normal day.'
But I'm asleep and first come the nightmares,
'combat or remain'.

IMAGINE GOING TO WAR

Goodbye, democracy. Hello pain,
glad I healed a wound with a certain friend.
Whatever I was, now what image is fastened on
 me?
Killing is survival but how can one truly thrive?

I'm studying a photo of a male opposer
he seemed to be saying 'Sorry'
whereas only 'kill' lay smothered on his lips
now he's comforting the almost extinct.

After the trenches overran with blood,
the soldier requested mental help,
yet only received a cell.
Now the person's postwar tensions
are welcome study for
the modern soldier's potential medicine.

ROLL THE DICE PLEASE, ONE MORE TIME FOR ME

Her suitcase is obtaining itchy feet,
wish I had burnt an image of myself.
The walls are still trembling from
the recent morbid phrases strewn around.
The cats started barking, too scared to come in,
there's more storms lurking around the house.
She's aching to pick up her belongings,
which are sighing with relief at living soon in peace.

I should have read your forecast in the leaves,
I should have been a better domestic man.
You always were the ace at being the bread winner.
I should have agreed at having children,
instead of basking in reams of five-star entertainment.
Now child's cries 'You're great Dad', shatter my fragile dreams,
we were competitors instead of a team.
I'll explore my greatest depths to repair your broken heart,
roll the dice, please, one more time for me.

Let's dig out and salvage our crumbling emotions,
otherwise arguments will flourish if we unite in heaven.

I have flushed you down the drain in many ways,
I hope to be the new man of this age,
by opening the door to unseen domestic chores.
I was never very good at loving anybody,
kisses equalled stalactites and embraces like ghosts.
My stopwatch for this relationship has nearly expired,
my mood will kill roses if I lose you now.

Romeo will never be my lucky shadow,
let me light the candle much more in you.
I'll unwrap my new self quickly now,
my old mind can rot in the garbage can.
We could report our happiest emotions in a scrapbook,
having children would expel the dire repetition
of loving the keys of the latest Jaguar.
Please, let's discuss our crossroads of despair,
remember we've melted each other's soul with kind words.

MONEY – MY RISE AND FALL

I felt really cool owning lots of money
and would laugh at low earners calling them dummies.
It could never happen to me any more,
I should change my bath water to champagne,
I did not talk much for time was money.

People whispered once I was too nice a person,
so I changed my ID without saying 'sorry'.
I had so many false friends,
so one gave out wrong addresses,
I did not trust anybody any more.

I was such a high flier,
excess then begun to bore me.
'It's a shame my wife is expecting,' I once thought,
'what time have I for a child?'
I'll just say, Hello 'It'.

So it really was a shock,
when life dared say I'd lost face.
My manager who owned less in life than me
said, 'Your behaviour's cost you your job.'
I felt I redeemed myself
by begging my surprised wife to stay,
we were two strangers bonded by love.

I admit I had to grovel
and sift through the mud
to surface with proper friends again.
My bank manager almost smiled saying, ‘You’re
broke.’
I thought my friends foolish
not to cancel my debts,
even though my next job would outsmart all their
money,
so I became a nice person again.

Money really wrecked my life,
it was hard work saving my soul.
I’m a low earner now ‘Hooray’
and I hold my face up high.
I do charity work, for this is my line.

I laugh at my high earning friends,
they think they purchase love with their money.
Many are in a lonely place
where I can understand them,
so I show them where not to fall.
My life beats their hour.

LONELY AND RARELY SAD, I THOUGHT

I was silently treading the City streets for loneliness,
the bars were alive, most eyes avoided my looks.
However the loners picked up on my stare,
we often end up too far down Memory Lane
and the rain falls down with much pain.
Yet I weep most for loneliness when in autumn time.

I enjoy shaking hands firmly with an imaginary Reaper,
by my favourite pond at sundown,
where we only discuss good things in life.
These meetings repair my sanity or perhaps loneliness.
The Reaper told me truths about myself,
so goodbye so-called friend, my only one is loneliness.

I bend down and feed City stray dogs,
one feels better talking to non-human beings,
it's brought back a light in my life once again.
Dog saved me from drowning in the canal,
I was lonely, drowning, it made me love people more.
Loneliness brings me happiness in my own personal way.

I felt rays of heaven when alone,
self-pity died in a bottle years ago for me,
yet life is full of comebacks.
Now I emerge to shake many human hands.
Yes, I do live in this world with other humans,
it's fun, it's sad, I want to share it not alone.

ACTOR'S MEMORIES

'Mean Streets' said the taxi driver,
my final act came four minutes before.
'History now' cried the Great Dictator behind
the door.
Mummy drags my figure into his tomb.
Inside Oscars turned to ash.
At my age, Welles had dried up too.

Fangs connecting neck, green man chases John,
ears aching toiling with the bells.
Antoinette on Scarlet's back, from the gallows.

'Juliet' – hand on heart – 'are you truly my girl?'
behind some mask I have played them all.

Autograph please – sorry – What's your role?
Sometimes I have gained acclaim and applause.
Brookshaw and the one-eyed creature,
the placard said it All.

OUT OF WORK

Webbs weaved on suit, the trousers are in a
jumble,
the cities full of snakes, heartbeats race.
My batteries were discharged one year ago.
Hello Mr Snail, knock, knock, is there anybody
there?
Who's next please on the assembly line?

Old Father Time stopped the clock – days dying,
thermometer explodes at 120 degrees in the house
– I'm suffocating
pondering at the cross roads – which path – no
I've lost my way.
An emergency – 10.20 – 10.40 – 11.00 I must
take a pill.
Joy, hundreds upon hundreds, lines of lies, tears
– all spill on that page.

Town people bustle past like a speeded up film,
Shop prices have multiplied ten times overnight,
you're living in the past – haggling's not allowed.
Head left – right – embarrassed, suspicious – I
feel like a spy.
Family and friends who've moved mountains
sometimes seem such strangers
My body's on that scrap heap 'Temporary basis'
Hope one million plus feel that theirs is too.

MESSAGES IN THE WEATHER

One must secretly bless nature's will
when the sun extracts you to dispose
of your irrational demons in the morning.
It strips away the segments of sadness
and leaves the core much easier to handle.

Many people positively adore it,
when vitamin pills are mentally rationed
until autumn boasts to the sun
'It's up to me to alter radically
people's moods to deal with hibernation.'

'Both of us should capture
an image of the sun
into a locket over our hearts'
said the lovers stargazing into each other's minds.

We would probably have crushed our days,
counting insects on our bedroom ceilings,
if our eyes had not mutually danced
when first meeting at the hazy pool,
which threw up dancing waves of passion.
Were we both hypnotised by the sun that day?

People acted like their ancient ancestors,
possibly predicting further trouble because
mankind's 'earthly' barbarity virtually blocked
    the sun.

Eventually the sun and moon
almost went on strike for one day.

'There may be unity for
further generations' the people cried,
for the words were sparkling across the sky,
'Don't squander peace on earth for greed'.
That really was a landmark time
when masses saw the most positive weather
    message of them all.

I CANNOT BELIEVE I NEARLY GAVE THIS AWAY

I'm lovesick for the train to take me home
to my wife and children who nearly banished
me.
I played Casanova with a younger lover,
my heart bled when love turned stale.
The rollercoaster, changing life and soul,
was too expensive a ride for me.

I was pardoned by my wife
for the rough childhood days I endured.
I pray to life for precious gifts given me,
I almost gave this away.
Life however, seemed charmed away from home,
reality was boring, I am always the little boy.

I, hand on heart, missed reading bedtime stories,
is the wife really coping, returning to work?
I feel like acting out penance for eternity,
my wife has rediscovered happiness for me.
I'll repay with promises lighting up bleak days.

My actions must be told when the kids get older,
for some of their childhood months were
damaged,
by a lonely figure intent on destroying lives.

In a nightmare my wife and children walked
away from me into rain, rejoicing in happiness.
I'd hate men if my children repeated this human
    curse.

Happy days have returned to this family again,
I play the fantasy games with the children.
I'm still a child who now won't run away,
the ex-lover has promised to fade.
My sanity became stale when
my family were for sale.
My mind's still angry, for I almost
gave this priceless happiness away.

LIVES ARE EASIER WHEN LOVE'S AROUND

Peter was ambitious and lived alone,
he thought it easier to catch
the silver suns on his own.
In his soul he thought he could breathe without love,
but his mind only takes him to areas
where he can only break down and cry.
Tears shatter louder on the ground when love is gone.

Peter sat down and wrote his first long letter
to brother where hearts and memories clashed
about the happy times and struggles they had together.
They mentally warned each other that,
aching heart meetings plagued their minds,
so they set a date where
handkerchiefs would not dry in the wind.
The rollercoaster of life would otherwise freewheel
where reunions are lost forever in grains of sand.

Peter wanted to become an ambassador to his parents,
where a younger voice in moments of frozen time,
would ease a troubled mind about growing old.
Peter swore to be one of their mirrors.

Love merged in new experiences in life,
so love always swore to survive,
for the sake of humankind.

Peter admits love has rescued his loner's mind.
Sacrifices were not bitter, he feels a younger man.
He thanks certain people for giving advice
on love which gave the courage to search.
Although some arguments seem like
winter never turns to sun,
new horizons are easier to catch when
there's someone real and you're both in love.

THE OLD AND TIME

I recently obtained strange vibes preparing for
Father Time
to usher in a hopeful memorable year.
I'm old, I feel like Father Time's Father,
yet I embrace the modern time,
my shadows do not yell for the past.

I lived with somebody before marriage in the
1930s.
I recently became my grandchild's age, 'Oh time,
stand still'
when he tapped into me for the timeless person's
advice,
on how two people survive before the blossom
springs.
The lost young adult is still ingrained in my old
bones.

I pierced open and entered my children's era,
by working in the new tidal trend wave – rock
and roll.
I have shed new skin,
I am the child within me.
I can move easily into other generation realms,
timeless should be stamped on my brain.

I've felt the sun shine much in my time,
yet recently omens change it to bleak skies.
My mask is tiring to appear trendy to the young,
I'll embrace old and still thrive for time.
Time breathes excitement, there's new horizons
for me.